SCRAP THE SCRUBS

THE NURSES GUIDE TO LEGAL NURSE CONSULTING SUCCESS

JANICE DOLNICK BSN, RN, LNC

Janice Dolnick BSN, RN, LNC

Scrap the Scrubs

The Nurses Guide to Legal Nurse Consulting Success

Janice Dolnick BSN, RN, LNC

Printed in the United States of America

First Printing 2019

First Edition 2019

Second Edition 2021

9798784293206

I dedicate this book to my fellow nurses who are the backbone of hospitals, clinics, doctors' offices and care facilities all over the world.

Thank you for all that you do.

Contents

Chapter One

Your Work Experience, Redefined

Leaping Head-First into the World of Legal Nurse Consulting

Clocking in at the hospital that day, all I could think of was resting. I had driven two hours in the dark. The lukewarm coffee I chugged on my way through the parking lot wasn't having much of an impact. My eyelids felt like bricks. I was drowning in exhaustion.

This wasn't just sleepiness. This was burnout.

I was a veteran nurse with a decade of experience under my belt, and plenty of practice fighting off fatigue. I genuinely loved my job. I had worked hard to get there, and while working as an RN in a variety of settings, it had been my dream for years to work in a hospital. From a bird's-eye view, I was at the pinnacle of my career.

So why was the pit in my stomach getting heavier and harder to ignore as the months flew by? I began to wonder if there was anything in store for me besides more work and longer hours. Would I ever know what life was like outside the demands of my job? Would I ever have the chance to start a family? If I did, would I have the time and energy to be a good mom?

Just before entering the hospital that dim morning, I finally admitted something I'd been ignoring and avoiding for too long: nursing would take up as much time and energy as I let it. To live the life I wanted, I would have to find some different ways of pursuing the career I love.

You can probably relate. You're likely a registered nurse with at least a few years of experience under your belt, a deep love of your job, and a creeping fear of burnout. You can't imagine leaving the medical community, but you also know that you can't keep going at your current pace.

I wrote this book to show you that there is indeed another path forward. Your experience as a nurse is valuable beyond nursing itself. It is particularly valuable to the legal community. Establishing yourself as a legal nurse consultant will allow you to keep one foot in the medical world while starting to live life on your own terms.

My career as an independent LNC started with a lot of trial and error. It culminated in 2009, when I founded my own LNC company, National Nurse Consulting. This book is the blueprint I was so desperately looking for all those years ago.

What is a legal nurse consultant?

Legal nurse consulting is a growing industry of experienced nurses who trade their scrubs for suits and lend their unique expertise to the legal community. Legal nurse consultants, or LNCs, are hired by attorneys who need advice on medically-focused cases, and work alongside legal teams in a professional relationship.

Your knowledge of the medical system is extremely valuable to legal professionals. How great is that? By working together, you can help attorneys and other legal professionals save time and money when they're working on cases that involve medical records of any kind.

Legal nurse consulting is often a revelation to registered nurses who have spent their careers focused intently on a single path. Who would have thought that you could step away from the hos and instead work from anywhere at any time for a variety of interesting clients and cases?

It's time to take the professional blinders off, blink a few times, and look around. Legal nurse consulting is an established and growing field, and a lucrative one at that.

But don't quit your day job just yet: you still have a lot to learn. No one becomes a legal nurse consultant overnight, but you can, and you will if you're ready to put in the time and energy required to learn how it all works.

From this point forward, I want you to stop picturing yourself as an employee and start thinking of yourself as an entrepreneur. This mindset will be critical as you start to learn and build your own LNC business.

The first few steps will be tough, but the process is worth the early effort. Once you've established yourself, you'll be able to work from nearly anywhere, and you'll get to choose when to pursue new business and when to lighten your work schedule.

Before you gain your first client as an LNC, your nursing experience will be your only calling card. Attorneys are looking to partner with registered nurses with significant experience in the field: to put it bluntly, you are only as valuable as the advice and insights you can bring to the table. If you're considering becoming an independent LNC, you should already have gained significant experience working in more than one medical specialty, and should be able to demonstrate expertise in your field.

If you're not there yet, that's okay. Keep growing and expanding your repertoire as a medical professional. It's a necessary part of the process, and I'll be here for you when you're ready.

But if you've got at least three to five years of experience as a practicing registered nurse, keep reading. I wrote this book for you.

Areas of practice

There are over one million lawyers in the United States. Not all of them try cases, and not all legal cases are medical-related. But a great many cases can benefit from your knowledge and experience as a nurse.

Getting Started in Legal Nurse Consulting: An Introduction to the Specialty, published by the American Association for Legal Nurse Consultants (AALNC), provides the following list of specialties that benefit especially from the input of LNCs:

- Medical malpractice
- Worker's compensation
- Personal injury
- Case management
- Billing fraud
- Social security disability
- Life care planning
- Product liability
- Corporate and regulatory compliance
- Toxic torts (or injury cases involving hazardous substances such as pesticides; a "tort" is a civil wrong)
- Risk management
- Healthcare licensure investigation

Why become a legal nurse consultant?

Working as a registered nurse in a traditional setting is stressful. Doctors are often too busy to be polite. Patients need your undivided care and attention, and don't always call for it in the most considerate terms. You're on your feet every shift, and finding time for a quick bite to eat can feel like a job in and of itself. I get it. I've been there and I remember those days very clearly.

It isn't unusual for nurses to feel overworked and underappreciated. From our very first shift we realize this is par for the course. Fortunately, I can tell you that the pace is less hectic and the pleasantries flow more easily when you're a legal nurse consultant.

As a legal nurse consultant, be prepared for entirely new work environments. You'll primarily be working from home, at a courthouse, or at a law firm. If you're anything like me, there will always be a part of you that misses the excitement and chaos of an emergency room, but your work as an LNC can give you a similar rush of excitement and you can still save lives, just in a different way. Your hard work behind the scenes and your testimony in court has the potential to determine someone's fate, granting them freedom or denying it.

For many nurses, becoming a legal nurse consultant is the beginning of living life on their own terms. The pressure is still on, and the stakes are still high, but in a different and often more manageable way.

If everyone's doing it, why should I?

"Isn't everyone becoming a legal nurse these days?"

"What can I possibly bring to the table that doesn't exist already?"

It's true that legal nurse consulting is a fast-growing industry. But here's the bottom line: there are plenty of attorneys, clients, and cases to go around. The job possibilities are all but endless if you're willing to hustle, stay focused, and prove your value.

If you're still on the fence, please keep reading. I know that once you finish this book, you'll feel encouraged to follow your dreams no matter how steep the learning curve it may be.

If you want to change your life, you need to commit to a plan and follow through on it. Now's the time to make that commitment. Pledge to yourself right now that this is something you want. As soon as I set my mind on becoming a legal nurse consultant, everything began to fall into place.

Attorneys want to hire you—they just don't know it yet

Since legal nurse consulting is a relatively young industry, many attorneys are not even aware of how useful and important your work can be. In fact, some attorneys still don't even know what a legal nurse consultant is or how they can help. And this is AWESOME…

A decade ago, when I launched National Nurse Consulting, most attorneys I contacted had never heard of legal nursing. At networking events, I would be met with blank stares as I explained to attorneys that I was a legal nurse consultant. The response was often positive enough, but too often ended with "I don't do medical malpractice cases."

I now use moments like those as an opportunity to educate attorneys on the value of LNCs. If medical records are involved in a case—which they are in a surprising range of situations—we LNCs can probably be of service.

Here's the real reason attorneys love LNCs: we're just as knowledgeable as medical doctors on matters pertinent to most cases, and much more cost-effective. While testimony in court from an MD is sometimes necessary, in most cases hiring a legal nurse consultant is a better use of an attorney's money and resources.

Once attorneys understand this, they will see your value.

Getting paid as a legal nurse consultant

I know what you're thinking: how much money do legal nurse consultants make? Can you still make ends meet?

The answer is yes, especially once you become established and begin to earn repeat clients. The more clients you get on your books, the more money you can make, simple as that.

Your hourly rate and retainer fee may vary depending on how many years you've been practicing as an RN, your location, and the size of the caseloads you work on.

One of the main benefits of being an independent contractor rather than a full- or part-time employee is that you get to name your rate. You can charge by the case or by the hour. It's now up to you.

While we're talking about money, here's a tip: don't rely on discounts and special deals. This starts a landslide of price competition and lowers the value of the service you're providing.

While you may be able to draw new clients by offering first-time discounts, the inevitable price jump will likely make them flinch when it comes time to consider hiring you again. Even a moderate discount tells your clients to value you less. If you insist on charging full price every time, you will be more valued and appreciated as a professional.

Setting your rates can be tricky. Do some market research online about the average fees charged by LNCs in the state or province where your clients will be based. An attorney practicing in California or New York will likely be bringing in bigger bucks than one based in Wyoming or Montana.

The bottom line is that you absolutely must do your research! Do not skip this step.

As a rule of thumb, the more money an attorney or law firm makes on a case, the greater the earning potential for you as a legal nurse consultant. A firm of more than fifty attorneys working on a class action will typically have set aside a bigger budget for your services than a solo attorney working on a small personal-injury case.

That said, it is completely realistic in many markets to charge upwards of $150 an hour.

Once you have a sense of the going rate in your market, aim high but be realistic. Attorneys are negotiators. Asking for too little will set the bar too low and present a poor impression of your abilities, and may cause problems in the future. Asking for well beyond the industry's average will earn you an automatic "no". You're an entrepreneur now: negotiating is part of the game.

Decide what your rate is going to be and remain firm about that number. Have a bottom-line rate that you're not willing to go below. Keep in mind that as an entrepreneur and independent contractor, you'll be paying more taxes and doing more administrative work (such as setting up and maintaining your business) than you were when you worked at the hospital. It makes sense to charge more than you might feel comfortable asking for at first: you're in a totally new industry, after all.

I often suggest that new LNCs get some formal accounting or personal-finance training. This can be a difficult skill to add, but since you'll be your own boss from this point forward, it's a crucial one.

Since implementing a fee schedule for my own business, I have never had anyone scoff at my rate. In fact, most attorneys comment on how much more affordable a nurse is over a medical doctor, and how much more help and information they receive for their money.

As an entrepreneur, you cannot compete based on price alone. There will always be someone to undercut you. Instead, focus on bringing the greatest possible value to your clients and on building strong relationships. People are more likely to buy from those whom they know, like, and trust.

The realities of entrepreneurship

Being an entrepreneur is not for everyone. Before you dive in to this new endeavor, consider whether you're truly ready to work for yourself. Test the waters a bit. See if you can find some hours during your work week to create a business plan, connect with attorneys in your network, or subcontract your services to an existing LNC business. It will be hard to achieve success as an LNC if you hate what you do, so give yourself time to dip your toe in and see if it's the right fit. However, if deep down your soul is screaming to get out of the bedside, diving in headfirst may be the only way to go. I was a head diver.

You don't have to go all-in straight out of the gate, but switching careers is a big commitment and things will get very real very fast once you quit your job and become a full-time legal nurse consultant and entrepreneur.

Weigh out the pros and cons. If entrepreneurship and freedom is what you want, there *will* be sacrifices to make and risks to take. This is true for all of us former RNs now working as full-time LNCs.

The benefits of running your own business are obvious, but like anything worthwhile in life, there will be ups and downs and you need to be prepared to stay the course when things get rocky.

When you become a legal nurse consultant, you will be leaving behind that sense of security that comes from collecting a regular paycheck and group benefits like health insurance and retirement plans. You need to consider how this will affect your finances and your family.

Then imagine the sense of freedom you will feel when you do take the leap and land your first client.

Not every personality is suited to building a successful legal nurse consulting business. Being an LNC requires compassion, organizational skills, the ability to think quickly and overcome obstacles, a strong work ethic, the desire to work long hours, psychological and emotional stability, the ability to communicate clearly and concisely, adaptability, a knack for problem-solving, and excellent attention to detail. If you check all these boxes, you're well on your way, and I do believe this industry would be a great fit for you.

Another vital element of becoming an entrepreneur is marketing. Once you launch your own business, you're no longer just an RN: you're now a marketer and a public-facing professional as well. You'll need a good supply of confidence to promote yourself and your business. That same confidence will come into play if you are asked to appear as an expert witness in court.

If you naturally have an outgoing manner, can maintain your composure under pressure, don't shy away from public speaking, and are able to form relationships easily, these traits will all work to your advantage as a legal nurse consulting entrepreneur.

Ready to get started?

If you have decided that starting an LNC business is for you, now is the time to commit to doing it right.

There are many things to consider when starting any new business.

One key to a successful launch is leveraging whatever resources are available to you during the planning stage. Whether you are a novice entrepreneur or you've had some experience in this area, consider visiting a small business development center (SBDC) in your area to see what they have to offer.

Business licensing, regulations, and other requirements and restrictions vary from state to state, province to province, and county to county. This is where your local SBDC can really help guide you when you begin setting up your business.

Most communities have an SBDC branch that offers free business advising services. To find an office near you in the US, visit: https://americassbdc.org/small-business-consulting-and-training/find-your-sbdc/; to find one in Canada, visit: https://www.ic.gc.ca/eic/site/csbfp-pfpec.nsf/eng/la03285.html.

These centers employ professional consultants who can advise you on the details of writing a business plan, bringing your idea to market, and expanding your business. They offer one-on-one counseling and training sessions to entrepreneurs in subjects ranging from business planning and marketing to accounting and financing.

NOTES

LNC registered nurses hired by Attorneys who needs ~~Med.~~ advice on med. focused cases, and work alongside legal teams (pg.2)

(pg.13) Legal nurse consulting occupies a space between two professions that rely heavily on professional certification.

(pg.4) Areas of Practice: Med. Malpractice, Workers Comp., Personal Injury, Case Mgnt. Billing Fraud, S.S.D., LCP, PL, Risk Management, Corp. and Regulatory Compliance, Toxic Torts, Healthcare licensure investigation

Chapter Two

Training and Getting Organized

"By failing to prepare, you're preparing to fail."
– Benjamin Franklin

Certification as an LNC is a mid-career goal that reflects your successful experience: it is not a requisite for entry into the field. Still, it's wise to decide early on whether you'll pursue some form of certification or training.

*Legal nurse consulting occupies a space between two professions that rely heavily on professional certification, but does not itself require a license or any other credential of your skills. That's not to say that you can jump right in: legal nurse consulting does require some education on the specific needs of attorneys.

I recommend exploring the many different programs and peer support options available to you before making an informed, confident decision on how to prepare for a career as a legal nurse consultant.

Whether or not you decide to pursue formal certification, I recommend highly that you find a great mentor. An experienced mentor can help launch your business, and can continue to advise you as your business grows.

As the old saying goes, it takes a village: attempting to switch careers without any sort of guidance will only lead to frustration and failure. You have a lot to learn—more than you know at this point—and a mentor can help you avoid common pitfalls.

In case you're struggling to find the right person, I offer a structured mentorship and training program that might interest you. Check out my free workshop [https://legalnursesrock.com/workshop/sign-up] for more information. Or you can visit legalnursesrock.com to learn more about out community.

If you choose to pursue formal certification there are multiple avenues available to you, however in good conscience, I can only recommend my own, which can be found here:

https://legalnursesrock.com/workshop/sign-up

Not all training opportunities lead to certification, and some are of dubious value. Wendie Howland of TheExpertInstitute.com, legal nurse consultant and editor of the *Journal of Legal Nurse Consulting*, has this to say on the matter:

There are several commercial companies that advertise courses of study to prepare nurses for LNC work... with several different sets of designations.

LNC certificate course through Legal Nurses Rock

I created the Legal Nurses Rock certificate program because other certificates out there did not prepare nurses adequately to take the next step in becoming a successful legal nurse consultant. The difference in our certificate versus the others available include:

- We found that other programs teach you the what of a legal nurse consulting but leave out the why and the how.
- Through our certificate/mastery program we teach you how to actually do the work of a legal nurse consultant by allowing you to work on real injury cases. Our team supplies video review of your completed work as well.
- By the end of the program, you will have real world work

product that you can send to an attorney to lan
first case. At the time of this writing, there is NO OTHER PROGRAM that does this.

To learn more about our hands on program please visit:

https://legalnursesrock.com/workshop/sign-up

Getting organized

Getting certified as an LNC is optional, but becoming a master of self-organization is not.

All successful business ventures are built on repeatable, reliable systems and processes. For LNCs, this means a formal approach to paperwork. LNCs work with large amounts of documentation, and your marketing and invoicing efforts will generate even more paperwork. To stay on top of your work and maintain a high level of quality and consistency, you'll need to organize your documentation in a way that ensures that everything's at hand and nothing's in the way.

The goal of any document-organization system should be to produce exactly the right document in less than a minute: that's the level of responsiveness attorneys expect when they contact you. A file cabinet full of clearly labeled, color-coded file folders organized by type, year, and case name is a good start.

My personal office file cabinet is divided into four main sections:

- Invoices and retainer contracts
- Client information (names, contact information, and areas of specialty for each attorney or firm with whom I've worked)
- Case-specific information
- Medical research materials (for example, frequently used or difficult-to-find statistics)

Over time, you can add new categories and sub-categories that reflect the sort of work you do. Some LNCs find that filing documents by case number works best; others prefer to start with alphabetized folders devoted to each client.

A disorganized office impairs your work as an LNC. Your invoices, retainer contracts, and work product can easily get lost in the jumble. Attorneys literally don't have time for that. Clients need to feel confident that they're working with an LNC who takes the job seriously, and that means taking time every week to focus on the administrative and organizational side of your business.

I've emphasized invoicing a couple of times in this section, and for good reason: if you don't bill your attorney clients in a timely manner, they won't pay you. It's as simple as that.

When I first started out as an LNC, I was so excited to have clients that I focused all my time on getting the work done and let the organizational side of things slide. It took me *two years* to get paid by one of my clients! That wasn't my client's fault. It was mine alone.

Please learn from my mistakes. Take at least one full day a week to organize your office until you're sure that you have exactly what you need, exactly when you need it.

Digital documents stored on your computer should be organized in a way that matches your paper-filing system. Many of my attorney clients hire me more than once, so I store their invoices and other pertinent information in a separate file on my desktop for easy access. Within each folder, you'll probably find it best to sort files according to the client's name or the date on which each document was last accessed.

Before you accept your first client, invest in a service or device to back up your computer's files and store them off-site in case disaster strikes. If that seems like overkill, remember that your clients back up every bit of data pertaining to their practices. Trouble does sometimes strike, and when it does, your clients will expect you to have taken the same precautions they have.

Much of your time as LNC will be spent working from an office, whether at home, at a client's office, or in a coworking space. But the job can also call on you to serve as an expert witness in court, if this is something you want to add to your behind-the-scenes role.

Before you launch your own business, it helps to get acquainted with your new work environment. If you're working at home, set up your office intentionally and spend some long stretches there even before you take on your first client, to make sure you have everything you need.

The same goes for courtroom appearances. All new legal nurse consultants should attend a few depositions **before** they are asked to be expert witnesses. Reach out to your professional network and see if you can connect with an attorney directly to ask about attending a deposition. This will give you a chance to see how the process works *before* you're deposed as an expert witness, which should take away some of the nervousness you might have about this very public side of the business.

Maintaining a positive mindset and building a supportive network

Imagine hitting the snooze bar at 6 a.m. on a Monday morning instead of trying to talk yourself onto your feet. That sort of freedom is exhilarating at first for new LNCs. But there's another side to the coin: freelance work can also feel scary and lonely at times, and it produces its own types of stress. So how do you maintain a positive attitude and clear frame of mind?

When you're just getting started, you'll be focused on hustling as hard as you can to land your first case, build some momentum, and start establishing a track record. But you should also take time to connect with other legal nurses who have walked the path on which you've just begun. Having like-minded peers to speak with on a daily or weekly basis is incredibly important for longevity in this business, both for emotional support and for practical guidance. Your network is truly critical to your success.

You may find a local group of fellow entrepreneurs that meet monthly at a local coffee shop. You may want to join a coworking space. You might even find other LNCs online. I run a private Facebook group for those that are interested in working with our team or are curious about learning more.

Our Legal Nurses Rock program facilitates opportunities for LNC entrepreneurs to connect with one another, share inspiration, wins, ask questions, and even travel together. Yes, we have had some pretty incredible yearly LNC retreats. You can join our Facebook Community here:

https://www.facebook.com/groups/legalnursesROCK

In this group, we share leads for opportunities, ask each other's advice on casework, and even just check-in with each other to make sure all is well.

It's much easier to stay optimistic when you feel emotionally supported and connected throughout this journey. Make a point of finding and joining a community as you begin your entrepreneurial journey and continue to nourish those professional bonds. When things get interesting, and they will, a solid network really makes all the difference.

NOTES

Chapter Three

Positioning Yourself Professionally

It's all in the details

As a Legal Nurse Consultant, your medical opinion matters. However, an LNC is only as good as their work product.

Work product is the way the LNC demonstrates to attorneys that they can gather and translate medical records into information an attorney can use to win their case.

How you structure your work product as an LNC will be the difference between working and getting paid or giving up your dream and heading back to the hospital.

Good work product will include:

- Fact summary report
- Medical chronology [with/without comments depending on the intended audience]
- Red flag identification
- Anticipation of opposing counsel's rebuttal summary
- Narrative summary
- Legal nurse opinion
- Next step recommendations

Unfortunately, there is not one size that fits all when it comes to Legal Nurse Consulting. You may be tempted to search for a "template" on google, but save yourself a lot of trouble and heartache now and just don't. Each attorney approaches their legal case differently. Part of the fun of being a Legal Nurse Consultant is discovering how you can serve each attorney client individually.

You wouldn't want a doctor to show up to perform a knee surgery on your MCL with an ACL template that she found on google... similarly, it's our job to recognize our attorney clients individual needs and cater our work product to fit them.

Your curriculum vita, also known as your CV or resume, and a letter of introduction will showcase your medical expertise to potential clients. Just as prospective employers did when you applied for nursing jobs, potential attorney clients may want to review your CV before they consider hiring you.

If you're planning to rock it as a legal nurse consultant, you need to start thinking like a business owner. You also need to consider how you will position and market your business in a professional and unique way. You're no longer an employee, you're now an entrepreneur. Every business needs its own unique brand that helps it stand out in the marketplace.

In this chapter, I'll show you how to create a winning CV and a letter of introduction that will translate your work as a nurse into the qualities that attorneys look for in legal nurse consultants. I'll also guide you through a few baby steps to start creating a professional brand for your business.

Details matter

Even if you have decades more experience than other RNs, your CV will not stand out unless it's professionally presented and includes all the right information. As nurses, we're trained to be detail-oriented. Legal nurse consulting is no different: just as at the hospital, details matter.

Your CV is your first chance to show potential attorney clients that you care about the details of their cases as much as they do. Make sure that every word is written and presented with intention.

Building a successful CV

In the previous chapter, we spoke about connecting with other LNCs and building a professional community. Now is a good time to ask a trusted and successful LNC friend if you can peek at their CV. This will give you an idea of what information you should include in your own CV, and how to present it. If you're at a loss for who to ask, you can also often find other LNC CVs through a simple google search or by using LinkedIn. We share multiple examples and video trainings inside of our programs as well.

Check out any job postings that law firms have posted for in-house legal nurse consultants. What are they looking for? What skills and experience do you have that overlaps their requirements? This simple bit of research can make a world of difference.

At all times, consider how you compare to the competition. Assuming you already have a CV geared toward your nursing career, you will now need to adapt that to your work as an LNC. Your history as a nurse and medical expertise is important: that's why attorneys need you!

Where have you worked? What did you do? What formal education do you have? What have been your most notable achievements? What specific skills and proficiencies do you offer?

Make sure to highlight all relevant legal nursing experience, and courses you have completed or certifications that you've earned. Include specializations and qualifications that distinguish you and present you as an asset to attorneys working on different kinds of cases.

Your CV should address more than just your career and education. You can also include information about internships, apprenticeships, certifications, teaching experience, or pro bono work. At the same time, make sure that your CV focuses solely on what you have accomplished in the medical and legal fields. To an attorney looking to make a quick hiring decision, anything else is just time-wasting filler.

You might want add a mission statement or a summary of qualifications that defines your unique selling proposition (USP), or what makes you uniquely positioned to assist attorneys as an LNC.

Some attorneys will want to speak to your references, however, it's common practice to leave those details off your CV itself, and instead to state "references available by request" at the end. If you have a long list of references and/or testimonials that you feel very confident in, you can include them in a separate document for distribution when you pitch your services directly to attorneys.

Alternatively, you can create a testimonials page on your website and include its URL on your CV (we'll cover your online presence in Chapter 5).

If at all possible, be ready to provide a reference from your supervisor at the last hospital you worked at as an RN (especially if you're a new LNC), or a glowing review from the last attorney you worked for (if you're a more experienced LNC).

Don't forget to ask your previous supervisors and clients if they would be willing to vouch for you. Negative feedback can derail your LNC business, so never assume what someone might say about you. Approach each potential reference first and ask for their blessing to share their information with prospective clients.

Once you've assembled your CV, review it critically. Are there any spelling or grammatical errors? Are you getting straight to the point? Are you providing measurable proof of your expertise? Is there anything you included that an attorney would consider irrelevant when selecting an LNC? Edit your CV, and then edit some more!

Design is another aspect of your CV to bear closely in mind. Here are some simple guidelines to ensure that your CV looks professional and draws attention for only the right reasons:

- Consider the overall look and feel of the document. What does your CV document say to you before you even read a word of the text?
- Use a simple, readable, and consistent font.
- Choose black or dark gray for the main text of your CV. Dark blue or medium blue can be used as accent colors such as titles and bullet points.
- Remember that your CV is not an art project. It's a business document that should convey your professionalism and expertise. Show personality, but always err on the side of professionalism.
- Are your margins ragged? Do you have too many hyphenated words that result in a messy look? Are there any drastic changes in font size that create a sense of imbalance?
- Don't be verbose. If you can make a point in a single sentence, do so. Attorneys are busy and want you to get to the point.
- Keep your CV under two pages. Focus on key points and career highlights. This is not an autobiography; clients can get to know you better after they've hired you.

If you're still unsure whether your CV is ready to send to potential clients, it might be worthwhile to hire a professional resume writer or editor to review the document and provide suggestions. They'll often find an improvement or two, but more importantly, the extra review will give you an extra bit of confidence as you pursue new business. To succeed as an LNC, you need all the well-earned confidence you can get.

Your letter of introduction

When you applied for your last nursing job, you likely included a cover letter that was customized to the position you sought. You'll be writing similar letters as an LNC, although we now call this document a letter of introduction.

When you become a legal nurse consultant, you will no longer be responding to online job postings; instead, you'll be reaching out to attorneys that you believe can use your services. You'll often be contacting attorneys cold, with no personal introduction from a mutual acquaintance. This is where a strong letter of introduction comes in to play,

Your letter of introduction should be customized to each attorney you reach out to. Here are a few tips:

- Focus on each attorney's unique needs. Start and end your letter of introduction with specific statements about how you can help them specifically. What can you do for them that no one else can?
- Research each attorney to whom you write, and get to know their practice well enough to tailor your letter to their areas of expertise.
- Make sure to include specific information about your background and experience that directly relates to the attorney's clients; demonstrate the ways that your expertise meets the attorney's specific needs.
- If possible (and if you have permission), mention other

attorneys with whom you have worked with on similar cases and who will vouch for you.

- Indicate that you're available for a brief informational meeting, either in person or by phone, so you can chat more about how you can be of service and answer any questions they may have.

As with your CV, ask a professional or a trusted friend to review your letter of introduction before sending it to a potential client. A small spelling error can put the kibosh on your other efforts, so this document must be perfect.

Once you're confident that both your CV and letter of introduction are as strong as they can possibly be, start sharing them! These are documents you will want to attach in any introductory emails to attorneys who may turn in to clients.

Branding basics

Starting a new business--even if you're its only employee—requires thinking about how your business will be perceived publicly and what makes it stand out.

You want to build your LNC brand intentionally and authentically. Think of the positive aspects of your personality and experiences that you want to convey to your potential clients. Your brand should attract your ideal clients, build trust, and help them get to know and like you.

Developing a solid brand from the get-go can help underscore the consistency that will eventually make you a memorable and recognizable LNC.

Generally, a brand consists of both written and visual elements that communicate feelings and ideas describing who you are and what you have to offer.

Expect to take some time to develop a brand you love, but don't let this step stop you from getting started as an LNC. Plenty of new business owners have no idea how they want to brand themselves. Heck, plenty of huge companies constantly rebrand and reposition themselves.

Branding will be an ongoing and important part of your business. As a new LNC, keep in mind that any logo or branding you share publicly will be noticed. Make deliberate, well-considered choices.

Consistency is vital when launching a new business. Ideally, your business name, website domain name and social media handles will all be the same, or at least very similar; this basic type of consistency helps build your brand while avoiding confusion.

Is your business name:

- Catchy and relevant?
- Easy to pronounce and spell?
- Unique enough not to be mistaken for a similar business?

Don't forget that your business name will follow you and grow with you wherever your LNC business takes you. Spend some time to decide on a name that feels right for you.

Making it official: buying your domain name

You may not be ready to build your website today, but one day soon you will, and you're going to need a domain name. Don't let this be an afterthought: it's an important part of your branding efforts, and changing domain names once your business is up and running can be tremendously costly.

To purchase and register a domain name you must go through a registrar. If you're not ready to actually build your website, but want to use a custom domain name for professional emails, you might consider a registrar-only service like the one offered by GoDaddy.com. If you're ready to launch a professional website, your hosting company can register a domain name for you as part of your subscription.

Choosing an appropriate and unique domain name with a business-friendly .com extension may take some research. While purchasing the domain name itself is a relatively intuitive task, finding the right name may not be so simple, since many desirable URLs have already been claimed by other businesses. If you don't already own your name as a domain (firstname+lastname.com), try to purchase it right now. This is the first step toward protecting and maintaining your personal and professional online reputation. If you've named your business something other than your name, look for that next. Registering a few different domains isn't overkill: you can always redirect one URL to another later. Ideally, your domain name will match your business name, or be similar enough to your that people easily associate the two. For example, a business called "Super ABC" could have the domain name SuperABC.com or ABC.com. In any case, choose a domain name that's memorable and accessible. You may need to try several versions of your business name before you can make your purchase.

Domain registrars will often suggest variations on names to aid you in your search. It's always best to choose .com as a top-level domain, but there are other options available: in a pinch, you might find that a domain name ending in .biz or .net is preferable to the compromises you'll need to make to find a domain name ending in .com.

Here's a tip that I wish I knew when I was starting my own LNC business. If you're not set on a business name yet, consider searching for your domain name first. An available domain name that makes an impact may just be the best basis for your actual business name moving forward.

If you have your heart set on a specific business name and the ideal domain name has been registered by someone else, you can check to see if it is actually being used for an active website. If not, it may be available to purchase from the registered owner. Some domain registrars offer services to help broker these deals, but keep in mind that you will likely pay a premium: chances are good that the domain name you're after has been registered by speculators who will only release it for a considerable sum. Be open to variations of your preferred domain name to avoid falling prey to these domain-squatters.

Once you register your domain, creating a business email address is essential to making your business appear credible. After purchasing your domain name, you will have the option to set up an email account through your registrar. It may cost a little bit of money to do so, but it's a worthwhile expense. Imagine handing out business cards at a networking event with your domain name and a Gmail address as the best way to contact you! That would be a red flag to potential clients that you're an amateur in running a business. The goal here is to portray the utmost level of professionalism, and that portrayal will require some upfront expenditures.

Your visual brand

Creating consistent visual elements is a critical part of building a memorable brand as an LNC. Once you have a logo designed, you can use it throughout your online and offline assets, such as in your social media accounts (see Chapter 4), your professional website (see Chapter 5), your email signature (see Chapter 7), and at events (see Chapter 9).

For example, my business is called National Nurse Consulting and my tagline is "Your Case. Your Success. Our Business". My logo incorporates each of these elements cleanly into a single identifiable brand.

We'll dive deeper into your online presence in the following chapters, but consider your social media profiles as key parts of your branding. Don't wait too long before reserving the names for your business-related social media accounts and using your logo to consistently start building brand awareness.

Ideally your business name, domain name, and social media profiles (Facebook, LinkedIn, Twitter, Instagram) should all be consistent. Grab your social media handles and domain name today before someone else does!

Here's a quick worksheet to get you brainstorming about your brand.

Possible Business Names:

✓ ______________________________

✓ ______________________________

✓ ______________________________

Possible Taglines:

✓ ______________________________

✓ ______________________________

✓ ______________________________

Available Domain Names:

✓ ______________________________

✓ ______________________________

✓ ______________________________

Available Social Media Accounts:

✓ ______________________________

✓ ______________________________

✓ ______________________________

✓ ______________________________

✓ ______________________________

Ideas for Visual Branding

✓ ______________________________

✓ ______________________________

✓ ______________________________

✓ ______________________________

NOTES

Chapter Four

Crafting Your Online Presence

Social media marketing for LNCs

Social media marketing tends not to be a major priority for us nurses, nor a particular strength. Sure, we spend time browsing Facebook and sharing pictures with our family and friends. But there's seldom a good reason to craft a unique social media presence when you're working tough shifts at the hospital, even if there were enough hours in the day.

However, in case you haven't noticed, social media these days is used for more than posting cat videos and birthday greetings. It's also an amazing opportunity for entrepreneurs to use platforms like LinkedIn, Facebook, Instagram, and Twitter to brand themselves, reach potential clients, and turn those clients into repeat customers.

Why LNC entrepreneurs need a social media strategy

One of the first rules of business is to always be where your clients are. While in-person networking is very important (see Chapter 9), the reality is that most of us are too busy to personally build a large and solid enough network to sustain our businesses. We're also all glued to our laptops and smartphones, for better or for worse. Social media is an amazing opportunity to reach out to busy attorneys and start to build your profile and client base remotely.

Social media platforms can also drive traffic to your website (see Chapter 5) as you begin to grow your business and brand. If you're already feeling overwhelmed , please take a deep breath with me right now. Let's do this together, one step at a time.

You don't have to be active on every single platform, every single day, straight out of the gate when you launch your business. However, you do need to begin building your presence online in order to compete with the thousands of other LNCs using these tools to reach clients and secure business. Let's start by looking at the most important social media tools for entrepreneurs.

LinkedIn

If you're just getting started with social media for business and personal marketing, start here. LinkedIn is the most popular professional social networking site in the world; as of the writing of this book, I believe that LinkedIn is the most powerful social media platform for LNCs.

Not only does LinkedIn act as an online CV and showcase your experience and skill-set 24/7, it's also a way to build your network, find new business, and become a thought leader.

Your LinkedIn page (here's a link to mine or visit https://www.linkedin.com/in/nationalnurseconsulting/) should include the same information that you have in your CV, but communicated in a less formal manner. The ideal LinkedIn profile includes your headshot, business information, branding, professional summary, details about your employment background and education, a list of your unique skills, testimonials, and contact information.

Always keep in mind that everything you present on social media reflects the type of work product that you'll be providing to your attorney clients. Make sure that your LinkedIn profile is complete and presentable. Treat LinkedIn as if it's the only thing that an attorney will see before hiring you, because it just might be.

You can and should post and share content on LinkedIn that's relevant to your ideal client. For example, you might link to articles of interest to your network, or sit down and write a blog post about LNC issues. Sharing content is a proven way to remain atop the minds of potential clients, build credibility, and display thought leadership.

Be sure to log in to your LinkedIn profile at least once a week. Before long, you probably won't need any reminders to do so: LinkedIn is a great tool for researching and connecting with potential clients and learning more about their businesses, their personal interests, and even their pain points.

In this business, like so many others, it's not so much what you know, but who you know. What makes LinkedIn such an amazing resource is that you can showcase who you are as a professional legal nurse consultant while also easily connecting with others who are active on the platform.

LinkedIn is like a cocktail party where everyone you could ever want to meet is in attendance. First you will want to connect with the people you know in real life, just like most of us gravitate towards friends at the start of an event. Before long, you'll be comfortable enough to make new connections by simply sending an attorney a short message introducing yourself. I recommend using the following script to connect with strangers who may turn into potential clients down the road:

Hi [First Name]. Hope to connect. Have a great week! ~ [Your Name]

That's it! You don't have to think of something clever or even send them any kind of sales pitch. You wouldn't do that at an in-person networking event, and you shouldn't do that on LinkedIn either. You simply want to start growing your network and building relationships so that you can take business conversations *off* the platform and into the real world through an email, a phone call, or an in-person meeting.

Once someone connects with you on LinkedIn, they will be able to see your full profile and any content you share on the platform. This alone will keep you on their minds the next time they need an LNC. You can also move things forward by sending them a message and seeing if they might be open to starting a business conversation.

A script for that sort of suggestion might look something like this:

Hi [First Name].

Thank you for connecting so quickly. Let me know if you're ever interested in chatting more.

Warmest Regards,

[Your Name]

[Your Business Name] / [Your Business Tagline]

Again, you're not sending them a hard sales pitch or making demands of them. You're simply putting yourself on potential clients' radar and making yourself and your business known.

Most of us love meeting new people, especially those who may be able to help us with our own interests. Your goal with LinkedIn is to demonstrate your professional value and expand your professional network with those who may have the power to hire you one day.

Facebook

As of February 2019, 2.23 billion people log in to Facebook every month, and 65% of those people use it daily. You read that right. Billions of people.

This means that you can reach many professionals on Facebook, including attorneys and other legal professionals. That is an opportunity that simply cannot be ignored.

Many attorneys get so caught up in their cases and trials that they don't reach out for help. I stay on their radar through a Facebook Business page [https://www.facebook.com/nationalnurseconsulting/] where I share content, and by running ads specifically aimed at attorneys. Maintaining an active presence on as many platforms as possible could mean that the next time an attorney requires assistance on their medical-related legal cases, you're the one they'll call!

Facebook also reminds previous clients that they can hire you again, and lets you connect with new attorneys in various legal specialties. It's another important step in raising your profile and building trust among your new professional community.

Once your Facebook Business page is set up, be sure to add your logo, tagline, location, and service offerings. This is part of creating a memorable experience for anyone visiting your business page, and building a recognizable brand.

Creating content for your Facebook Business page may seem difficult at first, but it's quite simple once you get started. Here are some ideas on what you can post about:

- How you, as a legal nurse entrepreneur, can assist attorneys in their work
- Important information that attorneys know but forget
- Important information that attorneys may not be aware of
- Other people's content that's relevant to attorneys (properly credited, of course)
- Information about an upcoming training event that you or a colleague will be hosting

If you're still stuck on what to write about, you can ask some trusted legal professionals in your network what they would like to know about and answer their questions before they even have to ask. Remember that any content you create for your Facebook Business page can also be used on LinkedIn, and vice versa.

Twitter

Twitter appeals to a slightly different audience than LinkedIn and Facebook, and has lost favor in some circles. But it's still a good channel for anyone looking to elevate their position as an industry thought leader. If you want to be plugged in to breaking news and connect with journalists who might be interested in interviewing you for a story they're working on about a case, Twitter is still the place to be.

A Twitter presence can help build your professional network, even if it doesn't provide much of a showcase for your skills and experience. If you're not interested in actively participating on Twitter, at least consider setting up a private account just for listening in, following others in the legal space, and watching for breaking news and trends that might impact your business. If you can spot a newsworthy item, you can share it with current or potential clients to keep your business on their minds.

Remember that you should add your Facebook, LinkedIn, and Twitter URLs to the following:

- Invoices
- Your CV
- Your letter of introduction
- Your business cards
- Your business marketing materials
- Your signature on professional emails
- Outgoing snail-mail business correspondence

- Comments that you leave on blogs by other professionals
- Any other social media accounts you may have

Using social media to build community

The fun isn't over! LinkedIn, Facebook, and Twitter are amazing tools for building your business, and I know from experience that using them regularly will help you achieve your goals.

Being a legal nurse consultant isn't always easy, and it can get lonely at times. One of the other great advantages of actively using social media is connecting with others. Whenever you find yourself feeling stressed or overwhelmed, remember that you can always reach out to other trusted legal nurse consulting entrepreneurs via social media, and they will likely be able to sympathize.

Don't delay this important step. Get active on social media and start building your presence, and your business, today.

NOTES

Chapter Five

Creating the Perfect Website

First impressions matter

While social media can help you connect with others in your field, the heart of your online presence should be an asset that you fully own and control. Your business website is an absolute necessity as it will attract potential clients, explain what you can do for them, and collect their contact information.

Why you need a website

To put it simply, owning and developing a website is a must if you want to be taken seriously as a legal nurse consultant and as an entrepreneur. While LinkedIn, Facebook, and Twitter are critical to developing your online presence, they are no substitutes for your own website. Think of your website as your home base and your first opportunity to make an impression on potential clients. It should encourage attorneys to get to know you, find out what you have to offer, and feel like they're working with a reputable, established professional.

A well-developed website allows your current and prospective clients to locate you quickly and gives your existing clients an easy way to refer their colleagues to you. A website can also act as a vehicle for collecting leads, sharing content, and providing samples of your work.

You'll have a wide range of options when setting up your business entity online. New products and services hit the market all the time, and today's best practices may not be tomorrow's. That said, you'll want to start with two basic steps:

1. Register a domain name if you haven't already (see Chapter 3 for more on this).
2. Select a host for your website.

Once you have chosen and purchased your domain name, you will need to find a company to "host" your website so that it can be published and available online for the world to see. You should be able to accomplish each of these steps through the same company: many domain registrars also offer in-house website hosting, and many web hosts have relationships with domain registrars that allow you to choose a domain and set up your web space in one transaction.

Of course, you can also register a domain using one service and buy hosting through an entirely different company. It all comes down to your budget and your comfort level with this more technical side of getting set up online. Different hosts charge different prices, typically on an annual basis. Popular web hosts as of this writing include GoDaddy, Bluehost, and SiteGround. Feel free to ask your fellow LNCs for hosting recommendations, or your web developer if you plan to use one.

Use a professional email address

As we discussed in Chapter 3, if you haven't already set up a professional email address, now is the time. This is a huge step toward establishing your professionalism as a legal nurse . It's hard to take an entrepreneur seriously if they are conducting business from a personal Gmail or Hotmail account.

For your email, you will want HIPPA-compliant formatting so that you can work with attorney clients who accept specific types of legal cases. HIPAA (Health Insurance Portability and Accountability Act of 1996) is United States legislation whose data-privacy and security provisions are designed to safeguard medical information. You cannot get this service through a free email service provider. Any established web host can provide you with appropriate encryption as well as the HIPPA-compliant formatting, but it's worth your time to confirm that you'll be getting what you need.

Encryption helps keep any information transmitted to you confidential and safe, whether that's information received directly from an attorney, or secondhand from their clients.

Website development: professional design vs. DIY

Most of us legal nurse consultants have wide-ranging skill sets, but building and coding websites is not typically among them. To create a website, most of us are wise to hire a professional website developer to ensure that the result looks clean and professional, and that it works as intended. Some good DIY options are available that let you create your own web sites (e.g. Squarespace and Wix), but I highly recommend investing in a professional job.

Remember that you will be competing with thousands of other legal nurse consultants nationwide, all of whom provide services identical or similar to yours. Every single one of the most successful legal nurse consultants I know have invested in professionally designed websites. If you want to compete for big business, you need to put your best foot forward. If you'd hire a professional contractor to build a storefront business, you should consider taking the same approach to your online presence.

Untold thousands of web designers and developers are capable of building the sort of web site you'll need, and each charges differently for their services. As a new LNC, you will likely not have a huge budget for your website, and that's okay. Shop around and find someone at a price point that you're comfortable with.

Your needs, from a coder's perspective, are relatively simple and straightforward. Your new website doesn't need every bell and whistle available, so don't be suckered in to paying huge amounts of money. Make it clear to whomever you hire that you simply need a website that incorporates current best practices, showcases your brand, and looks clean and professional. You also want to be sure your new website can grow with you as your business expands and evolves.

Are you a DIYer?

While I always recommend hiring a professional and staying away from the free website builders, I know that some folks are born DIYers who will insist on building their websites themselves. If you enjoy dabbling in this area and have some experience in website development, this may be just the project for you. For new LNCs with DIY ambitions but little coding experience, some affordable solutions are available that offer drag-and-drop-style website-building tools.

If you decide to build your website yourself, please remember that this is the first impression many clients will have of your business. Make sure that the result is something that you will be proud to share with your network, and that it serves as an effective calling card for new business as a legal nurse consultant.

Search engine optimization

Search engine optimization, or SEO, is the practice of writing and coding your website so that it pops to the top of search-result pages. You'll want to ensure your website developer (or you as a DIYer) is well-versed in the latest SEO developments. With solid

SEO behind it, your website will be among the first listed by search engines like Google when potential clients search for legal nurse consulting services.

A high-quality website development team can provide SEO services to help you maximize your website's visibility. Some companies even offer SEO-optimized copywriting services. The bottom line is that you want your website content to be easily discoverable while remaining engaging, informative, and easy to read.

What do I put on my website?

The next thing to consider is what pages and content need to be on your business website. Let's start by discussing your main page, otherwise known as your home page.

Throughout my years working with attorneys, I have learned that what potential clients really want to know is **what you can do for them**. They want this information as directly and quickly as possible. Your home page should fulfill this need while also showcasing who you are as an LNC.

Avoid cluttering up your home page with too much text. This can be overwhelming, and a disorderly website will reflect poorly on you as an LNC. Imagine it from an attorney's perspective: if your website is chaotic, what will working with you be like?

Above all, create a home page that conveys professionalism, intuitive navigation, and high-quality information. Then build the rest of your site around those same qualities.

Logical website organization

Visitors will land on your home page when they visit your URL, which matches the domain name you purchased. That first page should clearly explain what your business does and what you have to offer.

You will also likely create sub-pages that share more specific information, like your list of services, your areas of specialization, testimonials from clients, and contact information. Don't hesitate to add as many sub-pages as you need to tell your story. It's better to have a menu of well-organized pages than just one or two highly cluttered pages that try to do too much.

Common examples of sub-pages include:

- Home
- About
- Services
- Testimonials
- Blog
- FAQs
- Contact

Try to keep your top-level menu clean and simple: not every page needs to be listed on your primary menu. For example, a page to schedule an appointment with you should probably be on a subpage of your "Contact us" menu item.

Here is a link [ntnlnurseconsulting.com] to my own company's website, which was designed by a professional. Feel free to use it as a guideline when brainstorming the kinds of pages you need for your own professional website.

What content goes where?

Once you have decided which sub-pages to include on your website, you'll still need to organize your content and decide what goes where.

Here's a list to help you build your website in a logical manner. Feel free to add anything else that you believe is critical for your website's success:

Home:

- An introduction about you and what you have to offer as an LNC
- A call to action ("Contact me for a free consultation")
- Text and/or video explaining how you are different from other legal nurses
- Your areas of specialization
- Your phone number and e-mail address

About:

- Your professional biography and headshot
- A list of associations you're affiliated with

Services:

- A list of services you provide
- What types of cases you focus on
- What a client can expect when they work with you
- A call to action for a free consultation

Testimonials:

- Testimonials written by attorney clients

Blog:

- Your blog posts
- An e-newsletter subscription form

FAQs

- Questions and answers about legal nurse consulting
- Free resources or samples that showcase your work

Contact Us:

- Your professional contact information

- Your office hours (if relevant)
- An easy-to-use contact form

Make sure that your website provides all the information a potential attorney client might require. A properly developed website will be a 24/7 marketing machine working on your behalf, and will become your virtual home base as a legal nurse consulting entrepreneur.

Your website and your brand

Your website must be informative, but don't overlook the value of visual appeal and compelling branding. Design is important. Colors, fonts, and other elements combine to give visitors an overall impression not just of your website but of your entire business, and of you as a professional.

So what colors should you choose for your website? Work with your designer to develop an appropriate, on-brand color palette before getting started. The main color is important, but without the accent colors you won't know which colors to use for links, highlighted text, and other features.

Be consistent. Your website is an essential part of your overall branding, and it should be consistent with all the other elements of your business. Use the same color palette on your website and for your offline marketing materials like printed flyers and brochures. Reinforcing your brand online and offline helps people become acquainted and familiar with you and your business.

Select easy-to-read fonts and use them consistently. Even if you design and build your website yourself, advice from a professional graphic designer can go a long way to creating a look that reflects a professional image. This is all part of building a brand: a bit of initial investment can pay off quickly when it helps attract your first clients.

Maintaining your website

Regardless of how you choose to build your website, you need to plan how it will be maintained. Will you learn how to do this yourself, or will you hire someone to help you? Your website designer or developer may also offer a maintenance package and serve as your website administrator or webmaster. This is another question to ask before hiring someone to work on your website on your behalf.

A webmaster can be your long-term partner in keeping your website timely, secure, functional, and visible, even as the web-hosting landscape changes. A webmaster can also keep an eye on your analytics, which track your site's performance and identify opportunities to increase traffic. All of this encompasses the more technical side of being an entrepreneur, and is as important as the work you'll be contracted to perform as an LNC.

If you're not technically savvy and don't understand the inner workings of the internet, it's a good idea to develop a relationship with a professional web developer or webmaster and graphic designer to get your home base looking as professional as possible.

Just get started!

It's easy to get overwhelmed by all the decisions involved with creating your website. Don't let paralysis by analysis delay the opening of your business. This is a mistake I see time and time again, and it's a biggie. Nothing trumps experience as a legal nurse consultant, so get something online and get working!

From concept to launch and into the maintenance phase, consider your skills, interests and available time when you consider how to tackle creating your website. Reflect on your priorities when deciding on how to get started.

Remember that you can start with a simple, inexpensive website. This is just the beginning. Jumping in sooner rather than later will give you a better understanding of what you want to include on your website as your business grows. Most importantly, don't get bogged down with design decisions and technical concerns. Leave that to the professionals. Just get started…and don't forget to have fun with the process.

NOTES

Chapter Six

Blogging Your Heart Out!

Be a content maven

To blog or not to blog

Getting your website to the first page of Google's search results is a tall order and a worthy goal. It might not be your aim right now, but you can at least plan to get your site seen by more and more people, which will result in more and more business. The fastest and easiest way to accomplish this is through blogging.

Your website alone may not immediately bring you the clients that you want. However, including a blog on your website allows you to more easily build and manage a network of likeminded contacts and prospects. It also provides content to share on your social media platforms, which we discussed in Chapter 4 as an effective way to differentiate yourself in the crowded LNC market.

This is especially true once you have established yourself as a professional who is both an expert in the medical field and a trusted authority within the legal community. A well-written blog that includes the right LNC topics will demonstrate your expertise while persuading others to trust you and your professional opinion.

The more you blog, the higher you rank

Without due attention to SEO, your website will likely only be seen by those you directly ask to visit it. Your goal is to draw traffic while you sleep, attracting a stream of prospects to add to your marketing funnel. No matter how carefully planned or engagingly designed your website may be, your online presence needs the right marketing tools behind it.

Fortunately, you can include keywords in the text of your website and on your blog that will draw the right kind of traffic to you, and with it the right kinds of prospective clients. The more targeted your keywords are, the more ideal your site visitors will be after finding your page through a search engine, and the likelier those visitors will be to become clients.

Your search engine ranking will improve with each relevant blog post you publish. It's that simple.

Like it or not, most material published on the Web requires a relatively short attention span, and readers have adjusted their habits accordingly. Your blog should follow suit. Remember to add images to make your blog more visually appealing and less overwhelmingly text-heavy. Also consider posting items that feature lists, or that make their cases in a series of brief points.

Also consider creating fact sheets and downloadable templates or tools and sharing them on your blog. Resources like these encourage repeat readership, which is exactly what you're after. You'll get your page bookmarked and likely get your services booked as well.

Remember that plenty of attorneys are waiting to receive the information you have at hand and the expertise you have to share. Put it out in the world and see what happens. Just make sure that it's engaging, relevant, and enjoyable to read.

Tying it together: your blog and social media

Your attorney clients will get to know you through your blog, so be sure to post about a variety of topics that matter to them. What you write is important. You're the expert in your field, and attorneys may be looking for your medical knowledge when preparing for an arbitration or a trial. Be sure to mention your services occasionally throughout your blog, along with the reasons attorneys should hire you. Your website is yours, and you should use it to promote yourself while also providing valuable content.

When your content speaks to what your potential clients want and need, they won't be able to get enough of it. Regularly posting new content to your blog gives attorneys a reason to keep coming back. It builds trust and makes them want to contact you for more specific advice and information.

Don't forget to tie your blog posts back into your social media accounts. Share your posts on LinkedIn, Facebook and Twitter. This is how your content will spread and get seen by the right people. Others may even share your content with their own networks, multiplying its impact. You never know who might come across your blog and see your value as a consultant.

Along with consistently publishing solid content to your blog, you can improve your site's ranking in search engine results by including keywords in your posts that mirror the terms entered by searchers themselves. While you always want to sound like yourself and not a robot, using keywords in your blog posts will get the right people reading what you have to say.

How do you choose the best keywords? First, do some research. Find out which words are most commonly used by prospective clients who are looking to hire LNCs. Many online resources are available to help identify the best keywords for your niche, including the Google Keywords Tool and Keywoordtool.io. Write down the most relevant and popular keywords in your niche and remember to use them in future blog posts.

Many experienced bloggers begin with keyword research and use a list of keywords to guide their writing. Beginning with a list of keywords will help drive traffic to your website and help you decide what to write about.

Why you'll fall in love with blogging

Blogging is good for business, but it's also fun. Blogging offers you the opportunity to share what matters to you, your writing skills will inevitably improve, you'll raise your professional profile, and people will get to see what type of person you are and what you have to offer as an LNC in a way that a CV can't convey. Blogging can also be very social, particularly when you keep the tone of your blog light and friendly and leave the comments section on so that people can interact with your posts.

Everyone who visits your blog should leave knowing a bit about you and encouraged to contact you. Website and blog visitors who don't book your services right away can still become important contacts who refer you to new clients. Those who do hire you will appreciate having been able to get to know you online before trusting you with valuable cases. As long as you carve out a bit of time each week to keep your content fresh, there's no downside to consistent blogging.

Build a community of like-minded professionals and potential clients

Everyone has a handful of favorite websites that always seem to be full of useful resources. So why not create your own? By simply adding social media buttons to your website and blog, you can create a space for a community of potential clients to hang out. You'll have the opportunity to network with them and watch your social following expand.

How do you do this? Ask questions in your posts that compel readers to engage and share. Allow a section for comments after each blog post, and get ready to meet your public.

All you need to do to become a blogger is to share as much useful information about your areas of expertise as you can. I recommend publishing a new blog post at least every week or two. Do this consistently and you'll see your sphere of influence grow; your business will follow suit.

There are so many benefits of blogging: sharing your expertise, increasing your website traffic, building trust with prospective clients, attracting new business, even blowing off steam once in a while. We're lucky to have this opportunity to showcase our expertise, so don't let that opportunity pass you by!

NOTES

Chapter Seven

Email Marketing

Creating familiarity with potential clients

While the digital landscape is constantly evolving, email marketing remains one of the most effective ways to keep your current clients engaged, reach new clients, and build your brand.

New channels of communication are being introduced so quickly these days that it's easy to be lured into thinking you must master every new online marketing fad that comes along. That's not a good use of your time, and it will only dilute your marketing efforts in the long run. If you're looking for a proven way to drive measurable results, make sure you have a strong email marketing strategy in place before you tackle other channels.

According to the Direct Marketing Association, email marketing on average delivers a 4,300% return on investment (ROI) for businesses in the United States. Yet small business owners often assume that email marketing isn't effective, or that it's too hard to develop and maintain a winning strategy.

Many people assume you need hundreds of people on an email list to justify the effort. That's not the case. Email marketing is frequently cited as the most cost-effective form of online marketing for small businesses who do it right. These days, you can even automate and customize most of the process.

If you're new to email marketing, it may seem a bit daunting and complicated at first. Like anything else, it gets easier the more you do it. So jump in head first. You can do this, and you can start today.

A successful email strategy involves the following steps:

1. Build your email list and select your tools
2. Draft an email plan about what types of emails you will send
3. Design your email and create content
4. Automate, test and distribute your campaign
5. Analyze the results and tweak accordingly
6. Rinse and repeat!

Let's take a closer look at what you'll need to get started.

Build your email list and select your tools

Before you think about sending your first marketing email, you'll want to choose a system to collect and manage your email addresses, create and segment lists, and collect data so that you can adjust future emails as necessary.

With so many email marketing tools out there, you may feel overwhelmed at first. It's important to bear in mind that you can get started with any of them, and that you'll be able to make wiser decisions only after you've gained some experience. It's also important to remember that you can always move your list and email marketing campaigns somewhere else later on if you feel like you have identified a better option. Nothing is ever set in stone.

I recommend starting with an email marketing tool that offers a free or low-cost trial, so you can get your feet wet without a huge investment.

New tools become available constantly, but as of this writing here are some of the more popular options:

- Mailchimp
- Constant Contact
- Active Campaign
- AWeber

Mailchimp offers a completely free service up to a certain number of subscribers, but with limited customer support unless you upgrade to one of their paid plans. Constant Contact offers a free 30-day trial and is a popular choice for small businesses. You must pay for AWeber, but it's relatively affordable and very well-rounded.

Take a little bit of time to do some research and then just pick one and get started. Don't waste too much time and effort agonizing over the right decision before you get in there and develop a better idea of what works best for you.

If you're completely new to email marketing, you may want to check out a book that is specifically about that topic. Browse Amazon's bestsellers on the subject or visit your local library and just pick one to read. You don't need to become the most advanced email marketing expert ever; you just need an idea about how to set appropriate goals and how to achieve them. You can also check out the free tutorials offered by most email marketing providers. They want you to become a long-term customer, so most services offer videos with clear instructions that walk you through the steps of setting up your first campaign.

Consider adding a lead capture form to your website

While not mandatory, a simple signup form on your website that allows visitors to learn more about you and your services will help you build your list more quickly.

Consider adding an opt-in or lead-capture form in several places on your website, directing people to sign up to learn more about you, or to subscribe to your e-newsletter. This is something that your web designer can help you with.

Be sure to include text explaining what visitors are signing up for when they provide their email address. Include a form on your Contact page, but also on any landing page where you have an offer, and possibly on your home page as well.

If you have any plans for operating in Canada or in the European Union, make sure you and your webmaster comply with the GDPR (General Data Protection Regulation) guidelines. This regulation took effect May 18, 2018. Its purpose is to:

- support privacy as a fundamental human right
- require businesses that handle personal data to be accountable for managing that data appropriately
- give individuals rights over how their personal data is processed or used

Your email service provider should offer clear guidelines to help you comply with the GDPR, You can find the complete GDPR regulations at https://ec.europa.eu/info/law/law-topic/data-protection_en. Be sure to check the most recent US website requirements as well.

Building your email list

A quick way to start building your email list is to add email addresses that you have collected through your own personal networks, from previous clients, via professional associations, at networking events, and on social media. You must also legally always offer an easy way for your contacts to opt out of commercial communications if they do not want to continue receiving emails from you.

Continue building your list even when you think you have a big enough audience and plenty of leads. Collecting these addresses and leads for your business is not a one-time activity: it's an ongoing effort that will help you grow your business for years to come.

What's your plan?

Now that you've set your email collection machine in motion, it's time to decide what types of emails you will send.

Sending a monthly email newsletter is a good place to start if you have the discipline, time, and resources necessary to ensure that you publish consistently. You want to deliver real value to your clients and potential clients through these emails, rather than sending purely promotional messages. Mix in promotional messages with educational messages and even a bit of just fun stuff.

Consider including the following:

- Case studies
- General business announcements
- Interview with an attorney client
- Industry news
- Reviews of recently published educational works
- A summary of your latest blog post, linked to the post itself
- Notifications of educational or networking events
- Something fun and light but still relevant to your business
- Seasonal messages for holidays and special events

Make your email marketing appealing

Now it's time for the fun part! Almost all email marketing tools offer pre-designed templates to make sending attractive emails easy. You can use one of these templates or have one designed just for you. Don't overthink this part. As your business grows, you may want to invest in a full branding package whose email template matches your other marketing materials. When you're just getting started, it's more important to just get out there and get marketing.

Make sure that your design is mobile-responsive. As with your website, you want to make sure that emails appear appropriately on whatever device your reader is using. Ready-made templates from any major email marketing tool should have this functionality built in.

Be sure to keep your emails brief, professional, personalized, and goal-oriented. The key is to properly research the contacts on your email list before sending anything out so that the emails you send will grab their attention, make an impact, and remain in their inbox (and on their minds).

Segmenting contacts and customizing content

At first, you will likely be sending emails to a single set of contacts. As your list grows, however, you can start thinking about how you will categorize your contacts according to their interests, a process called segmentation. You can even create multiple contact lists to make sure you're sending the right marketing messages to the right audiences.

You may want to consider segmenting based on:

- Practice specialty (e.g. personal injury, criminal, malpractice)
- Geographic location
- Your current clients
- Your prospective clients
- Email engagement (subscribers who open all your emails vs. those who don't)
- Personal relationship with you

Include a call to action

Your emails should always include a call to action (CTA). A CTA tells readers what you want them to do after reading your message, and should include a button that sends readers to your website or social media account. Think about the actions you want your reader to take that are beneficial to your business. For example, you might want to ask readers to:

- Read an article on your blog
- Contact you for a free consultation
- Connect with you on LinkedIn, Facebook or Twitter
- Download a case study or free resource

Grab their attention

Take some time to consider each email's subject line. We all get hundreds of emails a day, and we ignore or discard many of them based on their subject lines. Think about what subject lines and content make *you* decide to open an email. Approach your email marketing with that same voice. Just like you, your contacts don't want to be sold to; they want to *connect*.

Automate, test and send your email

Before you send your email to your list of contacts, be sure to test it by sending it to yourself, and if possible to a trusted friend or business associate as well. You want to make sure that it renders well on a variety of devices (desktop computer, tablet, smart phone), has no spelling or grammatical errors, and is engaging.

It's always a good idea to have a second set of eyes on your email content to catch little quirks and errors. Remember, you're positioning yourself as a thought leader, and typos or boring content can derail that effort.

Once you have reviewed your email and made any necessary revisions, it's time to send it to your list. This can be a little nerve-wracking at first (it was for me!), but just hit Send and see what kind of response it receives.

Always include yourself in the contact list so you can see when and how the email actually appears in an inbox. No matter how diligently you test and review your emails prior to sending, there may be an occasional glitch or item you missed, and it's always best if you're the first person to spot the mistake so you can note it for next time or send a revised and corrected version of the email.

Analyze the results and tweak accordingly

Email marketing services provide you with the opportunity to analyze the performance of each message you send through a function called analytics. By getting familiar with your email service's user dashboard and its analytics capabilities, you'll be able to assess many key performance indicators (KPI) and determine how you might improve the results of your email campaigns.

Important KPIs to follow include:

- Open Rate: how many subscribers opened your email
- Click-Through Rate: how many subscribers followed a link in your email
- Conversion: how many subscribers completed a desired action
- Unsubscribe: how many subscribers opted out of your list after receiving your email
- Delivery: how many emails were successfully delivered
- Spam reports: how many subscribers reported your email as spam

Any good email marketing tool will share these analytics with you every time you send something out to your list. If you notice that certain types of emails are not being opened, or are not performing as well as others, you can look for ways to improve future campaigns.

Rinse & Repeat!

Once you have the process down and feel confident that you're providing your email subscribers with useful content that they want to receive, it's time to schedule regular email campaigns to stay in touch and remain top of mind, as professional marketers put it. You don't want to inundate your audience with too many emails, but you also don't want them to forget that they subscribed to your list.

Keeping subscribers regularly engaged with content of real value increases the likeliness that they will open your emails and respond to your calls to action.

Once you've gotten a handle on the email marketing cycle, you can automate large parts of the process. As long as you write compelling content, the business of crafting emails and sending them to appropriate contacts can be largely handled automatically.

For example, you can create an automated campaign with emails that are sent when an individual subscriber meets a predefined trigger, such as subscribing to your list from an opt-in form on your website. Your system can automatically send them a welcome email, then follow up a week later with an email containing links to your most popular blog posts. The following week, maybe you'll reach out to them to talk a bit about your services and your roster of happy clients. All without you having to do a thing. That's the time-saving genius behind email marketing automation.

NOTES

Chapter Eight

The Power of Thought Leadership

Author your own destiny

Once you get the hang of social media, blogging, and email marketing, you'll start to realize that you have a unique voice, an impressive library of content to draw from, and an extremely valuable LNC skill set.

Have you ever considered writing a book about your area of expertise? Publishing a book through a traditional publisher is no longer the only way to distribute your work to a worldwide audience. The ascendance of amazon.com and the emergence of other self-publishing platforms mean that anyone can share their expertise with the world.

Writing a book about your specific area of expertise marks you as an LNC thought leader. The very process of writing a book will also help you become a better communicator in general, which will help you advance as an LNC. It will also create an asset that you can sell, offering you the possibility of a passive income stream.

If writing and publishing a book sounds too daunting, keep in mind that times have changed. Getting a book published used to be a long shot; now it's something that anyone can do.

ebook vs. paper

If you're not ready to consider publishing a traditional bound book, consider starting with an ebook. You can even start by writing a very brief eBook that you make freely available for downloading on your website. Even a two- or three-page eBook can showcase your expertise and give you an edge on the competition. It will also help you grow your list of followers and act as a teaser to encourage potential clients to connect with you. eBooks also offer you the opportunity to include live links that send attorneys right back to your website.

Consider your book as another marketing tool. If you do decide to write a full-length book, it's best to have both electronic and print versions available: some of your audience will prefer reading on their devices, while others prefer the experience of holding a printed book in their hands. And some readers will be happy to buy both! Traditional publishers have tended to require the release of the printed book first, followed by an electronic version. This is no longer the only way to go, so do what works best for you.

Benefits of an ebook:

- Faster and less expensive to publish
- Faster and easier to share with others
- Immediate download caters to our need for instant gratification
- Busy attorneys are more likely to check out an electronic version on their devices while waiting for a meeting or during breaks from the courtroom
- Links from your ebook can take your readers directly to additional information

Benefits of a hard copy book:

- Visibility: a printed book on a shelf or the desk will keep you top-of-mind
- You can use a print book like a physical calling card, much like a business card
- Underscores your authority when displayed at conferences

and other events

- No need to charge up a device to read
- Some people prefer the tactile experience of holding a book
- For some audiences, a printed book carries more credibility than an ebook

Getting Started

Focus on a very specific niche: the more specific, the better.

A detailed outline will be your best friend. Prepare an outline with the major subjects you plan to cover forming the chapters of your book, then create a detailed list of points under each chapter heading. Set a schedule for yourself and try to commit to drafting a pre-determined portion of your book each week, no matter what. If you already have a blog, you can even re-purpose some of that content as the basis of your book.

Don't get discouraged before you start. Your book doesn't have to be long. It doesn't have to win a Pulitzer Prize. It just has to convey value to readers and offer a unique point of view.

Preparing to publish: invest in editing

Even if you were an English major or an award-winning journalist in a previous career, you need the services of an objective editor if you plan on publishing something beyond a few pages of work.

Even the best writers can be terrible editors of their own work. They know what they want to say, after all, and are naturally ready to make sense even of confusing passages, or to forgive grammatical quirks. A fresh set of eyes can more easily uncover basic typos and grammatical errors, along with broader issues of clarity, flow, and unity.

Lack of clarity is a common problem amongst books written by LNCs. Unclear references, ambiguous phrasing, and other errors of imprecision can confuse your readers. These types of errors may be particularly difficult for you to spot.

A good editor will also review your work for coherence and flow, which means moving from one idea to the next gracefully and logically. You don't want to lose your readers by skipping around and leaving them frustrated.

It can be hard to share your manuscript with someone else. It can be tempting to rush it to publication. And it can cost a bit of money to hire a professional editor. One way or another, though, your manuscript simply isn't finished until someone else has gone over it thoroughly.

Select a service for design and publishing

Whether you decide to publish your book as a paper volume or a digital edition, you need a great cover design and consistent, easy-to-read formatting. Some self-publishing companies offer design and formatting as part of their basic suite of services; some charge extra; some may not offer these services at all, and instead refer you to third-party designers.

Many options exist for publishing digital and hard-copy books. While I'm not recommending one service over another, here are few to check out:

- Amazon.com
- Standout Books
- Lulu
- BookBaby

Once you are a published author, whole new worlds open up to you. When your book is finally available, I'd love to hear about it. Until then, get writing!

NOTES

Chapter Nine

Networking in the Real World

Be you and be memorable

Conferences and other professional events are perfect opportunities to market yourself and your business. While you can get your new business up and running by following the advice found in this book and building a solid online presence, nothing replaces face-to-face interaction.

Do a little research to identify professional events in your area that you can attend either as a general conferencegoer or as an exhibitor. Join a bar association or business council to find out what's going on locally. Join bar associations in other states to help grow your network outside of your immediate area. Subscribe to legal magazines and keep a keen eye out for conferences. Bar associations and conference sponsors often have newsletters that you can join to stay informed of upcoming events.

Preparation is everything

Register for events early, and learn as much as you can about their organizers, speakers, and even their attendees. Most conferences publish lists of participants well in advance; use these to learn a bit about each speaker, so that you're prepared for a conversation when you meet them.

You don't need to dig too deeply here: it's easy these days to learn things about a stranger that don't quite fit into polite conversation. However, it never hurts to know about the general interests of key conference attendees; this will help you prepare an elevator pitch and decide how you will position yourself and your business when you finally meet.

Before you go, write down your goals for the event. These goals can be as simple as "meet three new people" or as elaborate as "secure a meeting with a decision-making attorney". Don't put too much pressure on yourself, but do keep your goals and accomplishments in mind as motivation to stay focused and to represent your business proudly and well.

Be sure to bring business cards, and mingle during breaks in the action. Along with attorneys, seek out paralegals and legal secretaries who may be tasked with locating appropriate resources for the attorneys they support. You never know who might be able to help you land your next client.

What do I say?

Instead of starting up a conversation with your sales pitch, try starting with a question instead. Ask about an attorney's specialty, how long they've been practicing, or where they practice. Ask if the attorney has ever used the services of a legal nurse consultant. If it feels right, you can then discuss how you help attorneys, stressing the benefits of working with you. Preparing an elevator pitch that you can customize according to your audience will help you feel confident and comfortable.

Craft your elevator pitch

An elevator pitch is a brief persuasive statement of no more than 20 seconds that you can use to break the ice with new contacts and build connections. Your elevator pitch should also include your unique selling proposition, or USP : what makes you especially capable of delivering exactly what each client needs. Consider the following steps when crafting your elevator pitch:

- Introduce yourself
- Explain what you do
- Communicate your USP
- Engage with a question
- Practice

It's as simple as that. For many people, networking feels awkward or even scary at first, and that's okay. Everyone is nervous! Just remember that networking is like a muscle: the more you use it, the stronger it will become.

If you find yourself struggling during your first couple of events as an entrepreneur, that's okay. Try making it more fun for yourself by turning it into a little game. Give yourself 30 minutes to share your elevator pitch with three new contacts. If you accomplish your goal, give yourself a small reward.

Another idea is practicing your elevator pitch ahead of time with trusted family members and friends. They can give you feedback, and you will get a sense of what works and what sounds clunky.

At the end of the day, networking is all about meeting new people, having fun, and providing value. As the old saying goes, "people will forget what you said, people will forget what you did, but people will never forget how you made them feel". Make everyone you meet feel special and heard, and watch your business grow in return.

Work that booth!

Some events may give you the opportunity to purchase a booth or a table to showcase your business and hand out information. Many conferences include dedicated spaces where exhibitors and vendors gather to meet attendees.

Think of your audience when you're presenting your services at an event:

- Who will be attending and visiting your booth?
- What kind of information do they want?
- How can you deliver information to them in a way that's unique and appealing?
- How can you make yourself stand out?

Find creative ways to stand out and bring more people to your booth. Everyone likes a freebie, even attorneys. Order some giveaway items printed with your company's name, logo, and URL; attorneys seem to love coffee mugs and tumblers. Items like these will most likely be used regularly, and will help keep your name top-of-mind. Attach a business card to your giveaways so your prospects can add your name to their list of resources.

Be Prepared

Invest in a professional sign and/or a tablecloth printed with your business name. Some events will include a sign as part of your registration, but some will not, so always bring your own marketing materials and be prepared to showcase your brand.

Here are other items you may want to consider for your comfort and convenience:

- A lightweight folding chair
- Drinking water and a healthy snack
- Breath mints
- Pads of paper and pens
- Chargers for your mobile phone and other devices

It's important to prepare in advance so you don't find yourself scrambling on the day of the event. You want attorneys to see you as poised, efficient, and confident; appearing harried and rushed might just ruin a valuable opportunity to promote your business.

Be friendly and approachable

Don't stand behind your booth quietly waiting for people to come up to you. Stand in front or slightly to the side of your booth and smile. Greet everyone who walks by your booth without launching into a sales pitch. Just be human and say hello!

Don't be discouraged if attorneys don't take the time to stop and learn about your services. They're probably just rushing off to the next session or to check in with the office. When possible, hand them a business card and flash a warm smile. That can be enough to prompt them to seek you out when they have a few minutes to spare. Be confident and don't be afraid to shine.

Get to know the other exhibitors. Other vendors work with attorneys, too, after all, and can be your referral partners. If they're aware of your services, they might just mention your name to their attorney clients who need your help. Just by striking up a conversation with a few of my fellow exhibitors, I've personally received referrals from insurance companies, bail bond services, and many others.

See if you can make friends with the event organizers as well. Offer to help set up or clean up. Sometimes they'll even extend a discount to those who pitch in. This also may lead to speaking opportunities for you down the road.

The magic of bar association events

One of the very best ways to secure new clients is by developing non-work relationships with them first. Attorneys do business with people they know, like, and trust. One of my favorite and most effective ways for building my successful LNC practice has been through local bar association events.

Take the following steps to get out there and get recognized as a leader and as the go-to expert at your local bar association:

Locate three local bar associations. Review their websites and look for the main contact person or administrator and a calendar of events.

- Call or email the main contact, introduce yourself, and inquire about the cost of becoming a member (yes, you can actually become a member).
- Ask about the cost of attending events as a non-member. If events aren't published on the association's website, ask for an events calendar as well.
- Show up! Be sure to bring your business cards with you, dress professionally, come with a smile, and be yourself. Attorneys are people too. Every month, plug into local bar association meetings to begin to build your network of attorneys. If you do this consistently, you'll see your business begin to flourish.

Promote your attendance

Use your website, social media and email marketing list to promote your presence at every event you attend. Be sure to check in on Facebook, post a couple of photos on LinkedIn, and share a great takeaway on Twitter. Announce that you're an exhibitor at the event and that you'll be available to answer questions about legal nurse consulting. This is a great way to connect with fellow attendees and increase traffic to your booth.

Offer your services as a speaker or panelist

Other than writing and publishing your own blog posts, content, and book, few things position you as a thought-leader quite as well as speaking at conferences and other professional gatherings.

Identify the event coordinators of conferences geared to the legal profession by scouring LinkedIn or by visiting their websites. Reach out to event coordinators as soon as possible to inquire about speaking opportunities. Event coordinators are eager to feature new topics and speakers, so don't be shy about putting yourself forward.

Prepare a pitch letter or letter of introduction to send as a proposal. This doesn't have to take a lot of time. Simply write down several topics that you feel you have the expertise to cover, and add copy points for each. Include a few summaries of stories or case studies illustrating each major point you're addressing. Make it interesting and engaging.

Once you get a nibble on your offer, work with the event coordinator to customize your presentation to appeal to the specific audience they're trying to please. This isn't an imposition: they will be grateful that you took the time to ask.

Once you're clear on your target audience, complete your presentation and practice until you have it down cold. Prepare answers for any obvious questions that may arise, and have a list of resources to share with the audience members seeking more information (including your website, of course).

After you deliver your presentation, take note of any questions or comments from your audience. This can give you great material for enhancements of future presentations and is a great source of topics to blog about.

While it may be nerve-wracking at first, becoming a go-to speaker about the legal nurse consulting industry can become an important asset in your marketing arsenal. Once you have one presentation down, you should be able to customize it quickly and easily for a variety of audiences.

NOTES

Chapter Ten

Never Stop Prospecting

Keep your funnel full and create an endless referral cycle

We have certainly covered a lot of information in this book. Start today on putting together all the pieces we've discussed and working on the tactics you've learned, and you'll be well on your way to scrapping your scrubs forever.

Becoming a legal nurse consultant is the most fun and rewarding decision I have ever made. Since launching my business, I've never looked back at an emergency room, and have even started a beautiful family that I get to watch grow by choosing my own hours and working from home. Now it's your turn to take the leap!

Start brainstorming business names, secure your domain, and get your website ready. Get out there with social media, email marketing, blogging, thought leadership, public speaking, networking, cold calling...whatever it takes.

Remember that these tools are not discrete. They all feed into each other to strengthen your business and are most powerful when they're used in concert.

Use the resources at your disposal

Meet a trusted friend for coffee and tell them that you're thinking of becoming a legal nurse consulting entrepreneur. Speaking aloud about your dreams can be your first major step toward turning those dreams into reality. Take at least one baby step each day toward establishing your business. Start to ask your former and current coworkers and clients for referrals and testimonials. These small but important steps can get the ball rolling and give you the confidence you need to dive head-first into your new venture.

At the end of the day, legal nurse consulting is all about credibility and referrals. I can't tell you how many referrals I've received simply by asking a couple of attorneys in my network to write a testimonial on my behalf. Every time I complete a case, I ask for a short statement about my services that I can post on my website. Never has an attorney said "no" to that request. Typically, attorneys are excited to write recommendations.

Remember the rule of reciprocity. Can you write a recommendation for someone in your network with whom you've worked closely? Could some of these contacts write one for you as well? It's human nature to reciprocate kindness. Maybe you were particularly impressed with how an attorney handled a case, how he treated his clients, how his staff worked as a team…these types of observations are all potential aspects of a recommendation that you can post on LinkedIn.

If you're just getting started and are struggling to get those first few testimonials, consider taking on some pro bono or volunteer work to grow your network and bring in recommendations. Get yourself out there, make some clients happy, and collect those testimonials.

Make your clients feel special.

Keep the contact information of all your clients and contacts in a customer relationship management (CRM) program or even just a spreadsheet. A well-organized list will let you sort your contacts in several valuable ways later on. Include clients' names, addresses, phone numbers, office hours, assistants' names, spouses' names, and even their birth dates. The best thing about knowing someone's birthday is that you can send them something small but special.

It may sound corny, but I can't tell you how many attorneys have brought me new business because I make them feel special and seen. I even get text messages with pictures of the gifts on their desks. This makes me smile since I know I helped to brighten their day.

As nurses, it's in our nature to make people feel better and I love that we can incorporate that into our business as legal nurse consultants. Make your clients feel special. They'll remember and take care of you when you do.

Join our community - we can't wait to meet you!

The community we've built at legalnursesrock.com is a strong and supportive network where you can find professional resources and share client referrals. Connecting with your fellow LNCs can bring you a considerable amount of work. When I get a lead for a case that falls outside my specialty, or my schedule is too full to accept a new case, I regularly subcontract work to Legal Nurses Rock members. Many other LNCs do the same.

Keep expanding your network

There is no excuse not to consistently generate new leads and referrals when we have all the resources we need at our fingertips.

It's as simple as using your favorite search engine to find attorneys who practice the type of law you specialize in. Hopping on social media, especially LinkedIn, connects you with attorneys in your area, which helps you keep adding potential clients to your list of prospects.

Of course, having a long list of leads won't do anything for you unless you reach out to them. Contact them by email or phone and ask for an appointment to meet and discuss your services. Use the elevator pitch you crafted in Chapter 9 to grab their attention. Send your perfect resume and letter of introduction. The key is to just keep working hard and making connections.

Develop your own procedure to systematically find and contact prospects and track their responses and your follow-up. This could be in a simple spreadsheet in Microsoft Outlook, a database program such as Access, or a more sophisticated CRM tool like Salesforce.

Keeping some type of record of your prospecting and outreach efforts will help you focus on next steps. Keep it simple at first and don't get overwhelmed with learning new software. Stick with what you know when you're just starting out, and just get busy growing your business.

It's all in the follow-up

Here's the reality: most attorneys you reach out to won't need your services immediately.

However, with the proper introduction and continued follow-up, you can make sure you remain top-of-mind when they or their colleagues *do* need your services.

Collect business cards from those you meet, and connect with them on social media. Send a personal note stating that you enjoyed meeting them, thanking them for their time, and offering to meet with them or schedule a call if they have any questions about how you might be able to assist them.

Building your relationships with attorney prospects through LinkedIn and other social media and email is great. But don't stop there. A traditional handwritten note will differentiate you from the competition and help you stand out. A piece of mail may also be seen and remembered by the attorney's administrative or paralegal support team, who can become valuable allies in your effort to gain new clients.

If an attorney you are speaking with doesn't have a need for your services right now, they may know someone who does. Attorneys know other attorneys, just as nurses know other nurses. Nourish the relationships you form so that prospective clients will remember you and stay in touch.

Many of my referrals have come from attorneys who have never used my services but have heard about me from colleagues. Regardless of an attorney's specialty, consider any new contact to be a potential source of referrals. Always show up with a smile, be diligent, follow the steps you've learned in this book over and over again, and watch your business grow.

Set your goals and keep your eye on the prize

"I don't want to work on Christmas Day this year. I want to be home with my family".

What do *you* want out of your life this year? Not wanting to work on Christmas Day was my very first goal for getting started as an LNC. Even before I was married and had children, I knew I would want to be home with my future family on holidays. I wrote the above statement on a piece of paper and put in my wallet so I would never forget where I'd been and where I was determined to go.

Make a list of goals and look at it every day. Keep it somewhere you can see it, like your bathroom mirror or refrigerator door. Everything you have striven for and accomplished as a nurse has led you to the right place, at the right time. You're on the verge of becoming a legal nurse consultant during the industry's infancy. You have the potential to bring more value to your clients than you know. Don't think of your marketing efforts as selling. Think of them as opportunities to educate people about how amazing legal nurse consultants are.

Be proactive and don't let rejections slow you down. Rejection is simply part of being the boss, so never take it personally. This is business. You're going to hear "no" more often than "yes". In fact, start thinking about how you can use the word "no" to sharpen your pitch and keep going.

You've got this. You really do. I believe in you.

My life changed once I stopped acting out of fear and started following my dreams. Stay positive and remember that you're in this for the long haul. Success doesn't happen overnight. Every little action you complete towards your goals adds up to success. A little progress each day can build your business into a strong, profitable enterprise.

I always remember the 90-day rule: *whatever seeds you plant now will likely not come to fruition for at least ninety days. Your business is like a garden. It requires daily maintenance to bloom.*

So, no more excuses. Here's to our success!

Come join us in the Legal Nurses Rock community at: https://legalnursesrock.com/workshop/sign-up

I'm living the dream, and I want you to live yours.

Are you ready?

NOTES

NOTES

NOTES

NOTES

Made in the USA
Middletown, DE
05 March 2023